Friar Park

HENLEY-ON-THAMES

1919
Estate Auction
Catalogue

Produced & Presented
by

Friar Park. Henley-on-Thames
1919 Estate Auction Catalogue

Copyright 2014
by The Cardinals

All Rights Reserved. No part of this publication may be reproduced, stored in a retrieval system, or transmitted in any form or by any means, electronic, email, photocopying, recording, scanning, or otherwise, without the prior written permission of the Publisher.

Limit of Liability/Disclaimer of Warranty: While the Publishers and the Author(s) have used their best efforts in preparing this book, they make no representations or warranties with respect to the accuracy or completeness of the contents of this book and specifically disclaim any implied warranties of merchantability or fitness for a particular purpose. Neither the Publisher nor the Author(s) shall be liable for any loss of profit or any other commercial damages, including but not limited to special, incidental, consequential, or other damages.

All reasonable effort has been made to contact the photographers and copyright owners of all images printed in this publication. Any omissions or errors are inadvertent and will be corrected in subsequent editions, provided written notification is sent to the Publisher. Many of the images in this book are transformative works and are protected by their own copyrights as well as the overall copyright protecting the contents of this book.

Many of the original images in this book are considered to be artistic renderings and should not be considered to be to scale or perfectly accurate. Various methods may have been used to determine areas for the floor plans. Any floor areas are approximate and may or may not exceed the usable area of the premises. Neither representatives of the Campfire Network, nor the Creators of this work have verified and make no representations as to (I) the dimensions of and/or the actual square footage of the premises, or (II) the exact location of various rooms and areas, or (III) whether the use of any room or area for the purposes shown (e.g. bedroom, kitchen, etc) complies with applicable laws.

The Campfire Network publishes its books in a variety of formats. Some content that appears in print may not be available in electronic books, and vice versa. The content of this book was generated during research for the paperback book "The Friar Park Scrapbook" by The Cardinals.

For information on this, or any other books, published by the Campfire Network, or for bulk & wholesale orders, or to schedule interviews with any of the Authors, please contact Cardinal@CampfireNetwork.com

Disclaimer: This publication is neither associated with, nor endorsed by, The Beatles, Apple Corps Limited, or Sir Paul McCartney, Ringo Starr, the Estate of George Harrison, or Mrs. Yoko Ono Lennon, as successor to the Estate of John Lennon.

Disclaimer: "Ye Friends of Friar Park" is neither associated with, nor endorsed by, The Beatles, Apple Corps Limited, or Sir Paul McCartney, Ringo Starr, the Estate of George Harrison, or Mrs. Yoko Ono Lennon, as successor to the Estate of John Lennon.

Acknowledgements

After having received such a favorable reception upon the publication of "The Dakota Scrapbook," which contained historical text recreated verbatim as they first appeared 100+ years ago, we were encouraged to believe that other texts and images of a similar nature might prove to be welcome on other subjects, such as Friar Park. As a result of the generous assistance of private collectors around the world who willingly shared their treasures with us, we had been afforded the opportunity to prepare and present this special edition which adheres to the design and layout of the original publication. Differences of opinion will certainly exist as to whether or not we succeeded in creating a respectful representation of the original 1919 version, but we feel the advantage of this book existing as it is outweighs the alternative of 1) this book not existing at all, or 2), a typical reproduction of the original book with nothing added nor subtracted. We hope that readers appreciate the additional effort that was made to create a special book.

The Publishers and Authors hope that this book, as with others of similar interest, will prove to be part of a handy and valued compendium to those interested in Architecture, History, Horticulture, Friar Park, and, of course, The Beatles.

Over the course of conducting research for this book we founded **"Ye Friends of Friar Park"** which is a Society of those who share our affectionate enthusiasm in Friar Park. Together we have quite likely gathered the largest collection of images, text, and information on Friar Park than anyone else in the world, with the possible exception of those who have inhabited Friar Park in the last ten+ decades.

The Publishers wish to thank **Servi Stevens** for his generous consultation during the development of this project and for offering access to his treasured collection of Friar Park memorabilia, and specifically for providing his copy of the original 1919 Sales Catalogue which was reproduced in order to create this book.

Special thanks also go to **Gerhard Bohrer** for sharing his priceless Friar Park collection as well as his valuable feedback and shared enthusiasm for all things concerning Friar Park.

We also want to express our sincere gratitude to **Krystian Pazdzierski** for providing the time and talent needed for such remarkable vintage photo restorations. Truly remarkable work! Further thanks to Claude Hitching, Jack Perry, Steve Silberberg, Dara Sperling, Darren Davis, and D.C. Blackbird for their time, talent, friendship, and feedback. We would also like to acknowledge the dozens of Beatles and George Harrison fans, Historians, Architects, and others around the world who have shared their photos, illustrations, trivia, information, and memories. A special thanks goes to Mr. Andrew Alpern for his many useful observations, which can not be too highly emphasized, and for being the inspiration for the serious study of various aspects of architectural history.

Despite all the contributions made from so many people, from so many sources, the responsibility for any errors, omissions, misinterpretations, or shortcomings anywhere in this book remain ours alone.

FRIAR PARK, HENLEY-ON-THAMES
1919

NATIONAL BUILDING RECORD
31, Chester Terrace, London, N.W.I.
WEL. 0619.

Solicitors:
Messrs, ASHURST, MORRIS, CRISP & Co.,
17, Throgmorton Avenue, London, E.C.2.

Land Agents:	Auctioneers:
Messrs, LOFTS & WARNER	Messrs, SIMMONS & SONS,
130, Mount Street	Henley-on-Themes, Reading,
Berkeley Street, London, W.I.	and Basingstoke.

FRIAR PARK ESTATE Particulars.

LOT I.   Coloured Red on the Sale Plan.

The elaborately designed and substantially built Country Residence, magnificently placed on a peak of the Chilterns high above the Ancient Borough of Henley-on-Thames, within a mile of the Station, whence London is reached in an hour, and known as

FRIAR PARK,

Commanding unrivalled views of the finest Thames Valley Scenery,

including the FAMOUS REGATTA COURSE, the Park Place and Hambleden wooded slopes, and the beautiful undulations of the Stonor Valley.

THE HOUSE,

erected in 1896, by the late Sir Frank Crisp, Bart., who occupied it as his Country Seat, is of highly diversified Gothic detail borrowed from the Pays-Bas where so many records of this period were recently destroyed by the Huns.

The main Garden facade has, combined with the Gothic detail of the low countries, been strongly influenced by the French Chateaux period as exemplified in the Dormer Windows and Tower.

FRIAR PARK ESTATE
THE APPROACH

is guarded by a lodge of similar design with heavy iron entrance gates which open on to a drive flanked by undulations richly ornamented with artistically laid out plantations and skirting the ornamental water which forms a distinguishing feature of the grounds.

The Decorations of the House,

both internal and external are based upon the decorative principle of the Friar which are met with at every point. Moveable noses of Friars switch on the electric light and Friars hold electric lamps. The Capitals of the pillars supporting the Hall shows Friars engaged in sleeping, dreaming, snoring, yawning and waking, in fact Friars abound in profusion on all sides. Some with ordinary faces on one side and sculls on the other, some drinking, some cooking. A pilgrim Friar welcomes visitors at the entrance, while on each side are statues of two Friars illustrative of the narrow and broad way. A scullery Friar watches over that portion of the House and Friars' faces decorate the Gargoyles. A Goblin Friar on the East side is depicted devouring two boys, while overhead is a Friar blessing, while on the North front Friars represent the four winds of heaven.

A reference should be made to the Sculptures in the two vertical side rows of the east front which convey double meanings such as the illustration of

"The Maiden's Prayer—(A Match).

Byron's apostrophe of modern Greece, " 'Tis Greece, but living Greece no more"—(A Box of Bear's Grease), and

"Who is the prettiest?" with the only possible answer furnished by "You are"—(A Ewer).

THE HALL

THE BILLIARD ROOM

FRIAR PARK ESTATE

This unique residence is entered by a

Vestibule or Outer Hall

20ft. by 10ft. 6in., on the walls of which are two Aphorisms:—

" Scan not a friend with miscroscopic glass;
You know his faults, then let his foibles pass.

— — —

" Life is a long Enigma." True my friend,
Read on, read on, the answer's at the end.

The East wall is decorated with three sets of Frescoes.

The Jacobean Centre Hall

has dimensions of 36ft. by 35ft., with a lofty height to the coffered ceiling of 37ft. It is

Panelled in Richly Carved Oak

the foundation of the idea of decoration being based on Shakespeare's King
Henry VI, Part 2, Act ii, Scene I.

A Vestibule at the North-West end leads to the

RICHLY CARVED OAK STAIRCASE,

A feature of the Hall is the beautiful coloured glass window at the North end.

An elaborately carved encircling Gallery is supported on Corinthian carved Oak Columns.

The spacious Fireplace is harmoniously designed.

FRIAR PARK ESTATE

The Suites of Reception Rooms

on the East front overlooking the best available scenery comprise

A Grand Dining Room

34ft. by 22ft. by 12ft. 6in., with a Window Alcove 6ft. by 6ft.

The ceiling is of heavily beamed and sub-divided Oak. The specially designed fitments include a richly carved Jacobean Sideboard, a fireplace of similar design with a delicately carved Inglenook and entrance door all in fine Pollard Oak. The available wall space above the Oak Dado is filled with specially designed embossed and gilded leather.

Illustrations in Tapestry

of two critical events in English History illustrating the DELIRIUM OF KINGS (I) depicting the Execution of Charles I, the other " The signing of the Declaration of Independence in America," adorn the North wall.

The Library

22ft. by 15ft. 6in. by 12ft. with fitted Bookcases, and the

ADJOINING STUDY

17ft. 6in. by 14ft. by 11 ft. 6in., are pleasantly placed between the Dining Room and the

THE DINING ROOM

THE DINING ROOM FIREPLACE

THE DRAWING ROOM FIREPLACE

THE DRAWING ROOM

FRIAR PARK ESTATE
Suite of Empire Drawing Rooms

which comprise an Ante Drawing Room 23ft. by 22ft. by 13ft. with two deep recesses; a fine pair of Satinwood entrance doors, carved in the Italian Renaissance detail give access to the beautifully designed

DOUBLE DRAWING ROOM

with well balanced dimensions of 42ft. by 23ft. with three recesses, the largest of which is 12ft. by 11 ft., the height of each room being 13ft.

The Two Exquisite Italian Fireplaces

are in carved alabaster, the ceilings and walls being decorated with highly ornate low relief plaster work and painted panels.

This beautiful Room is lighted by TWO FINE BAY WINDOWS on the East front and a large double window at the North end leading to a Garden Alcove with steps descending to the famous Caves and an approach path to the ROCK GARDENS.

A passage from the Vestibule and Grand Hall communicator with the Coat Room and Lavatories and leads on to

The Spacious Billiard Room

with panelled Dado and handsomely carved Fireplace, 35ft. by 18ft. 6in. by 12ft. occupying a position on the South-West front with a very fine circular bay window.

The floors of the whole of the foregoing rooms are in solid Oak.

FRIAR PARK ESTATE

A Carved Oak Staircase

leads to the Gallery supported on Corinthian Columns giving access to the

Suite of Rooms on the First Floor

which commencing from the North end of the Corridor include

A FINE GUEST BED CHAMBER, 22ft. 6in. by 19ft. by 12ft.

with

DRESSING ROOM, 15ft. by 11 ft. 6in. by 12ft.

A BEDROOM, 20ft. 6in. by 15ft. 6in. by 11 ft.

A well-appointed Bathroom and Lavatory complete this Suite. Adjoining, on the East side, are:

A BEDROOM, 22ft. by 16ft. by 9ft. 9in.

A SMALLER ROOM, 16ft. 9in. by 14ft. by 9ft. 9in.

BOUDOIR, 21ft. 6in. by 15ft. 6in. by 9ft. 6in.

LARGE BEDROOM, 22ft. by 18ft. by 11ft,

with

DRESSING ROOM 18ft. 6in. by 14ft. by 11ft,

and a good BATHROOM.

FRIAR PARK ESTATE

The West side of the Gallery leads to

THE MATTERHORN ROOM used as a Study,
11 ft. 6in. by 10ft. by 9ft. 9in.

A SMALL LIBRARY 20ft. by 13ft. by 9ft. 9in.

THREE BEDROOMS, 15ft. 9in. by 13ft. by 9ft. 9in.
18ft. by 10ft. by 9ft. 6in.
14ft. 6in. by 13ft. by 9ft. 6in.

THE BOOK ROOM, 17ft by 16ft. by 9ft. 6in.

Day and Night Nurseries, an additional Bathroom, Housemaids' Offices, and three W.C's complete the accommodation of the first floor.

ON THE SECOND FLOOR THERE ARE

9 Bedrooms, Tank Room, Bathroom, Linen Room and Maids' Workroom.

The Tower Rooms comprise a fine Workroom and a Bedroom.

In addition to the Central Staircase there are two Staircase approaches to the upper floors from the servants' offices.

Excellent Servants' Offices

are replete with every modern equipment and include:

BUTLER'S PANTRY, 16ft. by 13ft. by 13ft.

KITCHEN, 25ft. by 17ft. by 13ft.

THE DRAWING ROOM

THE MAIN STAIRCASE

FRIAR PARK ESTATE

LARDERS.

SCULLERY, 18ft. by 17ft. 6in. by 13 ft.
HOUSEKEEPER'S ROOM, 18ft. 6in. by 13ft. by 10ft. 6in.
SERVANTS' HALL, 18ft. by 14ft. 6in. by 10ft. 6in.
There is a LIFT to the top of the House.

There is extensive and sufficient Cellarage.

The House is provided with Central Heating, Electric Lighting, water from the Henley mains and drainage in the Henley sewers.

The Unique & Famous Gardens

with surrounding grounds encircle the residence and comprise a total area of

62a. 3r. 26p.

(partly within the Henley-on-Thames Borough boundary and partly in the parish of Badgemore, in which latter parish the house also stands), their distinguishing characteristics being

The Famous Rock Garden,

said to be the finest in the United Kingdom, laid out under the direct supervision of the late owner. Upwards of 23,000 tons of rock were used in the construction of this wonderful garden, in which is to be found practically every known specimen of rock plant, the beauty of which has

SECTION OF THE ROCK GARDEN

THE GNOME CAVE

THE ALPINE GARDEN WITH VIEW OF THE MATTERHORN

FRIAR PARK ESTATE

attracted thousands of visitors. A great feature of this portion of the grounds is a reproduction in miniature of

The Matterhorn.

The Beautiful Ornamental Water

forming a most attractive foreground, of the lovely and far reaching views from the house and lawns, ornamented by artistic bridges, curiously-designed stepping-stones, overhanging plantations and water caves. A lovely Japanese garden and pretty summer-houses add to the attractions of the surroundings.

The Far-Famed Caves

provide, under the rays of electric light, a fairy-land which has been the surprise and delight of many thousands. Here will be found the Ice Cave, the Vine Cave, the Wishing Well Cave, the Skeleton Cave, the Illusion Cave and the Gnome Cave, all fitted with harmonious representations of their nomenclature.

The Wonderful Group of Gardens,

including the Topiary, or Dial Garden, copiously ornamented with numerous sundials of almost every known design; the Herbaceous Garden, the Garden of sweet smells and savours; the Mediaeval Gardens; the Elizabethan Herb Garden, Nebuchadnezzar's Garden; the Rose Garden; the Rhododendron Glen and Rose Rookeries, all replete with the finest varieties and specimens of suitable shrubs, plants and flowers, and providing an intellectual entertainment, pleasing to the mind and eye, as one passes from one to the other.

FRIAR PARK ESTATE

Commodious and well-designed ranges of

Conservatories & Fruit Houses,

with a well-appointed

KITCHEN GARDEN,

add to the completeness of the attractions of Friar Park, which stands out as a unique specimen of a Country Home within 40 miles of the Metropolis.

The Coachman's Lodge,

with Stabling, Coach-Houses, Garage and enclosed Yard, and

The Garden Lodge,

in the centre of the southern boundary, complete the Lodge accommodation.

Other outbuildings include a well-appointed

Engine House

with batteries and accumulators, providing Electric Light for the premises.

Portions of the grounds include

Convenient Paddocks

of good pasture land, the whole being set out in the following Schedule:—

THE LOWER LODGE / GATE HOUSE

VIEW FROM FRIAR PARK

FRIAR PARK ESTATE

LOT II. (Coloured Blue on the Plan)

The Brick & Stucco-built & Slated Premises known as

"OXFORD LODGE,"

with PADDOCK,

comprising a total area of

10 a. 2 r. 2 p.

and containing the following accommodation :—

On the GROUND FLOOR :—

Entrance Hall leading to Three Reception Rooms, a Large Kitchen, Pantry, Scullery with Large Sink, and W.C.

On the FIRST FLOOR :—

Four Bedrooms, Box Room, Bath Room with Cold Water only laid on, and W.C.

There is a very commodious Cellar.

The Kitchen overlooks a Small Lawn which leads to a

FRIAR PARK ESTATE

Garden well stocked with Fruit Trees,

and to the Paddock beyond.

There is a convenient side entrance on the right of which lies an

Extensive Range of Outhouses

brick built and slated, comprising Stables and Coach-houses with Lofts over, and there is a small rough shed on the left-hand side.

This portion of the property is let to Mr. Henry Wilkins, on a yearly Lady-day tenancy, at a rent of

£50 per Annum,

Tenant paying rates.

The remainder of the land, which has a separate approach from Hog Lane, has been utilised for many years as Allotment Gardens, the rent of which was devoted by the late owner to local charities. This portion of the Lot is let to the Henley Town Council on a yearly Michaelmas tenancy, the rents derived therefrom amounting to the nominal sum of

£34 13s. per Annum.

OUTGOINGS :—Henley Tithe £4 9s. 9d.   Land Tax £3 7s. 8d.

FRIAR PARK ESTATE

LOT III. (Coloured Yellow on Plan).

A Very Fine Residential Site,

comprising an area of

7 a. 3r. 17 p.

with a South aspect and an excellent approach from the Henley and Badgemore Road, about a mile from Henley Station, and available for the local Water, Gas and Sewer mains.

This Lot is well ornamented with Ripe Plantations, and commands, southwards, extensive views of beautiful country scenery.

OUTGOINGS:—Henley Tithe £3 6s. 0d.

FRIAR PARK ESTATE

LOT IV.

A Similar and adjoining Lot

comprising an area of

6 a. 1 r. 36 p.

OUTGOINGS :—Henley Tithe £2 14s. 2d.

LOT V.

A Similar and adjoining Lot

comprising an area of

8 a. 2r. 1 p.

OUTGOINGS :—Henley Tithe £3 11s. 2d.

Lots 3, 4 and 5 are sold subject to a condition that not more than one residence shall be erected on each Lot, such residence to be of a minimum value of £2,000.

THE TOPIARY GARDEN

THE DUTCH GARDEN

FRIAR PARK ESTATE

SCHEDULE

NO. ON PLAN.	DESCRIPTION	ACREAGE
147	House, Grounds, 2 Lodges, etc.	21,072
42	Lodge Grounds, etc.	16,701
41	Lake	963
9	Pasture	8,182
148	Ditto	3,373
40	Rough pasture	632
155pt.	Woodland	139
126pt.	Park Land	11,131
145	Woodland	623
140pt.	Ditto	100
		62,196

The Well-designed & Handsome Boathouse with Small Lawn on each side,

occupying an exceptionally fine position about 50 yards above the famous Regatta winning post and commanding from the balcony a view of the whole Course, will be included in this Lot.

The Accommodation includes:—
A Wet Dock, 45ft. by 9ft.; a large Boathouse, 48ft. by 18ft.; a Workshop, 30ft. by 5ft.; a small Hall, with Dressing Room and two W.C's.

Above these on the first floor are:—A fine Dining Room, 28ft. by 21ft. by 14ft.; a spacious Landing; Scullery; Ladies Dressing Room; Kitchen, 17ft. by 13ft. by 8ft. 6in.; W.C.; etc., the Dining Room leads on to a Balcony which overlooks the river and beautiful scenery opposite.

The approach to this Boathouse is from the lower end of New Street.

OUTGOINGS:— Henley Tithe £26 9s. 6d.; Land Tax 3s. 6d.
There is a Thames Conservancy annual Charge on the Boat-house of £1 5s, od. for rent of Piles and Slipways.

OXFORDSHIRE.

Particulars, Plan & Conditions of Sale of

The Friar Park Estate,

Henley-on-Thames,

including

FRIAR PARK,

(the seat of the late Sir Frank Crisp, Bart.,) with its

Exceptional Grounds & World-Famous Rock Garden,

comprising together

62 a.   3r.   26p.,

together with

The Well-Appointed Boathouse with Summer Rooms

on the Famous Regatta Course; also in separate Lots,

"OXFORD LODGE," with 10a. 2r. 20p.

within the Borough, and

THREE GRAND RESIDENTIAL SITES

covering an area of 22a. 3r. 14p., on high ground above the town, within Badgemore Parish,

which

Messrs. SIMMONS & SONS,

in conjunction with

Messrs. LOFTS & WARNER,

will offer for Sale by Auction, on the Premises, on

Saturday, August 9th, 1919, at 3 o'clock p.m., in 5 Lots.

Solicitors:-	Land Agents:-	Auctioneers:-
Messrs, ASHURST, MORRIS, CRISP & Co., 17, Throgmorton Avenue, London, E.C.2.	MESSERS. LOFTS & WARNER, 130, Mount Street, Berkeley Square. London, W.I.	MESSRS, SIMMONS & SONS, Henley-On Thames, Reading, and Basingstoke.

www.ingramcontent.com/pod-product-compliance
Lightning Source LLC
LaVergne TN
LVHW061326060426
835510LV00017B/1943